Fresh Start
For Homeowners

Avoid the permanence of foreclosure
and secure your future with a
Fresh Start in *four steps or less*.

*Finally explained in a way
that's easily understood by ages seven and up*

ISBN-10: 1453874607
EAN-13: 9781453874608

"Good judgment comes from experience, and experi-ence…well, that comes from poor judgment."

- Cousin Woodman
(Popularized in its later adaptation by Will Rogers)

Intro to
Your Fresh Start = FIVE AND
ONE-HALF HOURS

· · ·

Could you spare that much time to protect the rest of your financial life? A study by the National Association of Mortgage Brokers (NAMB) found that seven out of ten home owners who needed help because they could no longer afford the payments on their loans were not even raising their hands and asking for help. In our experience of helping home owners for years, the biggest challenge is the fear that comes with not knowing what to do and the paralysis caused by imagining what it will take to get there.

If a lack of knowledge of what to do and the time it will take has kept you from improving your housing distress, then join the club of people who no longer have an excuse. Now you can feel confident going for a loan modification by applying the secrets the pros use, or you can do a short sale and increase your chances of it closing from 10-15 percent to 80-90 percent. You can avoid foreclosure while getting a Fresh Start and moving on without sacrificing much of your precious time at all.

We'll show you how right here; *Fresh Start* offers you everything you need to know. Whether you are a first-time home owner, or you are a seasoned real estate investor, you can use these tools to exercise your best option. We're not going to tell you that you'll be done and at your destination in five and one-half hours because that's not reasonable. But in as little as five and one-half hours of focused study and mindful work as you read the following pages, you will be able to chart a course to where you want to be. It's been said that *all you need in life is a specific destination and a great start, and the rest (the middle) will take care of it-self.* You choose your destination, and we'll provide the great start and help you along the way.

You can dive right into the work you came here for using our industry leading forms, worksheets, step-by-step instructions, and invaluable insight or start with some theory and background motivation with the intention of sculpting your *why* to get you through any *how*.

INSIDE YOU'LL FIND:
- Five of the simplest, most effective Worksheets, Tables, and Forms to cut time while ensuring it's done right the first time.
- Four sets of Turn-by-Turn instructions from where you are right now to where you want to be, with great tips and suggestions along your way.
- Six "Sarah's Tips," which are the personal accounts of what was done (some right but most wrong) along a journey of starting fresh that she made alone. She shares her experience so you don't have to make the same mistakes!

- Sixteen Pitfalls – Traps that you **will** encounter along your way…and most importantly, how to circumvent them.
- Four of the most powerful mental and practical exercises you can invest in either before, during, or after you begin this process to help you get further, faster!

Are you ready to give yourself the gift of a Fresh Start? In as little as five and one-half hours of focused study and work, fueled by the simplicity of putting one foot in front of the other. You owe it to yourself to take your first step right now. - The authors

Table of Contents

• • •

Preface

. . .

In any amateur approach to a weighty subject, the perils can be obvious. Yet there is one advantage: you are not expected to be loyal to the expertise you have otherwise studiously acquired and you are not relegated to the same devices that have dominated the landscape up to this point.

Of course, amateurs rarely succeed. We offer the shortcomings of the following in all of its brilliance and eventual faults as an example. We are obviously ignorant of most of the intellections required of a competent lawyer, real estate attorney, tax professional, or a bearded pirate treasure hunter☺. While not formal, we are students of the subject and at least reasonably well versed in the subjects we discuss. But what will be evident to anyone who has studied such matters is how truly untutored we are. We offer nothing more than our experience—which could be the classic error of the amateur.

How then, can we defend this venture?

Our research and development phase of writing this book was anything but. It consisted of us rifling through nearly every book online and on the shelves of our local stores that attempted to fill the huge gap of information "out there" and bring it to the living rooms across the country. While all pieces of work we consulted were clearly aiming to be comprehensive, timely (as their publishing dates made clear), and inextricably valuable, there was still a huge piece missing—*connectivity*. Going through this material can feel like being dropped in a foreign country where you don't speak the language and everyone has had too much to drink! If this work was to be done, it needed to be a *Fresh Look* at an old phenomenon that's been in the recesses of every neighborhood, forever. I hope that right now your thoughts are echoing ours when we began this project: "The last thing anybody needs is another book with a point drawn out over hundreds of pages when it could've been made in ten." However, we were inspired by the experiences of helping hundreds of families in our Free Hope|Against|HOPE Home Ownership and Foreclosure Prevention Workshops over the last two years.

This work afforded us a unique perspective that seemed to differ from the one represented in the books already out there: the people's voice. After all, as Theodore Roosevelt said, "Nobody cares how much you know until they know how much you care." The voice of the people was undernourished and needed a container that they could touch, feel, understand, and most importantly——USE. In our experience, help required two parts: (1) the content, yes, but also (2) the container. Margaret Atwood has said, "Context is all." She meant that there is no truth without context. And unless you were a full-time practicing real estate agent up on all the latest and greatest or a lawyer who specialized in the field, the help was buried inside a context that was largely indigestible. So while the content was rich, it lacked the container, the connectivity…the voice.

We took our workshops to the heart of communities where distressed owners most needed our help, and we used a grass-roots, town-hall meeting approach. What we learned from those owners was passed to us as the gift of their collective need. As much as we endeavored to help everyone on a one-to-one basis, it wasn't possible because the need was so great. We found that we could do just as much good sharing our assistance to small groups. So the workshop was born. Our next challenge came when the need surpassed a small-group setting. So we entered the webinar realm. Next came the challenge to share our knowledge with people beyond our locale. That led to this book.

We are aware of the book's shortcomings, and there may be some of which we're unaware. But our purpose is clear, whole, and complete. It is no different here than it has been since the day we raised our hands to be community leaders in this overarching challenge—**whether we like it or not and whether we are even**

aware of it, we are ALL either part of the growing problem or part of the growing solution. So, all apologies now delivered, we invite you to these thoughts, these ideas, and these workable plans of action that are part of this journey to achieve your Fresh Start. We hope (and expect) that you will be rewarded with everything you need to accomplish that and in doing so, reward us with the knowledge that we chose wisely in devoting this part of our lives to you. We could ALL be part of the movement toward the growing solution.

Now you may be asking yourself, who in the [insert explicative of your choice here] are these guys, and why are they qualified to speak to me about what I am going through? Here's our story.

Jesse's Story

. . .

(Take a deep breath and walk lightly with me because this is the first time I've ever put this down on paper. I found the courage to share my story embedded in the hope that we can somehow begin to understand each other through sharing.)

"Financial distress, shattered dreams, foreclosure, forced to play the hand dealt, and somehow always make the best of it—I have lived with these themes, these challenges, and more importantly, these feelings since I was thirteen. We're always told that we would learn more from our failures than our successes, and I'm sure that works for adults…but try telling that crap to a kid who is just being pulled along on someone else's ride. My story isn't unique, and we're watching this scenario being played out in the hundreds of neighborhoods across the country right now. In fact, as you read this, with unemployment, foreclosures, and overall financial distress and disorder at record highs, the number of people living Jesse's Story is multiplying exponentially. What could be unique, however, is how early and often the pattern presented itself in my life, and what I chose to do about it.

This story picks up steam in 1990, when I was thirteen. Forged out of the humble beginnings of a blue-collar family, my older brother and I had a mom who was a struggling local artist and a dad who was a self-employed contractor. We were all suffering severely from two things: a nasty, rainy winter that left the whole county out of work and our father's life-long struggle with alcoholism was peaking. To make matters worse, that November, we lost our mom to cancer. We didn't get much of a warning—we had only learned of its arrival six months earlier. This was the tipping point for my family's barely functioning financial situation, and it immediately disintegrated into total despondency. I hadn't even stepped foot in high school, and I was on my own. Looking back, it was amazing how fast it happened. I was young, but somehow already asked to be old. And within months after losing my mom, my dad was suicidal and withering away. My brother was away attending his third year of college while I was weeks away from losing my home and about to be ALL alone. At the eleventh hour, a ray of light crept through the darkest of those rainy, winter clouds; his name (ironically enough) was Ray. Ray Simpson was an unlikely beacon of hope because he was an ambulance chaser of sorts. Ray was just a local guy who had money and a rather unique business model of taking advantage of people in financially distressed situations. See, back then, it wasn't the whole housing market in distress, just us. Our home still had some equity in it. So his offer was simple: "I'll catch you up by paying the amount you are behind (which at that point was about three months). You pay me back, plus interest, in one year, or I take the home." We were desperate, so my dad took the deal.

As luck would have it, the rain cleared up and offered the starving county's outdoor workers some reprieve. My dad was able to get back to work, catch up with Ray, and get back to making the minimum monthly obligations for the time being. I was disoriented and in survival mode at the time, but when I look back I realize that Ray's intervention affected the course of my life. We didn't know that option existed, and had Ray not appeared FOR us, the course of my life would have been very different. Ray's small intervention allowed us to sidestep county programs and foster systems in my formative years, enabled me to stay in school, and kept me from being uprooted from my friends and my community. For the first time in my life, I was forced into a space where I had to ask myself, "Am I going to be bitter, or am I going to be better? It was my defining moment. Despite my youth and disorientation, I had a moment of clarity. I made a silent promise that no matter what happened, I was going to choose better. I wasn't going to **be** economy, alcoholism, cancer, or foreclosure; I would **be** a Ray for somebody else.

See, later in this story of my dad getting caught up on the house payments and avoiding foreclosure, something else caught up with him as well: alcoholism. The demons of the disease took the best of his judgment, and he attempted suicide a few years later. *Attempted* suggests that he was unsuccessful, and that's only partly true. While his time here wasn't done, the attempt took a big part of him…and me with it. It left him permanently disabled, and the blast left him relegated to a life without, among other things, sight. His attempt led me to take a leave from college, return home to help out with everything, and figure things out. There I was at the proverbial crossroads once again. Was I going to be the victim? Was I going to let this define me? Was this going to make me bitter or better? I found hope from an unfamiliar source. He was an old friend who just emerged from total obscurity, now well traveled, and experienced in the arts of healing the common pains of human life. He found me alongside the proverbial road with a broken wing and nursed me back to flight. He introduced me to the idea of healing from within. He surrounded me with a supporting environment of health, walked me from the bitter place I had chosen by default to "better." This time was special, though, because this time it was by choice. I invested that time in myself, got my affairs in order, helped with what I could, and saw myself back in a college classroom by the next semester. His name wasn't Ray, but I was beginning to see the pattern emerging.

Fast forward to 2007, when the world as we knew began to crumble underneath us. All the rules that I thought I could play by were no longer available, and I found myself in the crosshairs of victimhood once again. This time, it was *my* home. Without enough income to support the responsibility I had taken on or loan options to bail me out or equity to sell, I had to do the one thing that I was most scared of in this life. I had to go back and stand toe to toe with the one memory that has haunted me since I was that vulnerable boy who's future was to be determined by foreclosure. You could say I looked for the "ray of light," and you could say that there was none to be found. I had to let my home go to foreclosure.

It was at that moment that I decided I was going to do something about this that was going to make a difference. Maybe I was channeling that promise I had made to myself as a boy or maybe it was my way of dealing with my own loss. Whatever it was, it was a commitment to never being defined by my circumstances. Choosing not to identify with the victim, the person who *has a foreclosure on his record forever.* It was Maya Angelou who said, "When I know better, I do better." Here we were again—bitter or better? What I needed at that moment was another ray of light. Someone who could've helped me make a more educated decision based on what my real options (not just the ones the banks were giving us). Now, it was now my turn. I decided it was time to be that Ray, to "do what I could with what I had where I was." Along with my friend Cherie Tiscareno, who was experiencing the same thing in her community, we created a not-for-profit organization. It was to be a collection all the information we could learn from the folks out there who were raising their hands and making a difference. Our aim was to arm them with the tools of change so that their honest mistakes made trying to get ahead didn't permanently disable their future. Over the past two years, Cherie and I have selflessly given our time, tools, and acquired expertise in service to anyone who had one hour to spare to come to one of our Hope|against|HOPE workshops and receive the forty-five-page Tool Kit we hand out. This book is the extension of those collective experiences. Where those workshops left off, this book picks up. The truth is that the one hour was only enough to go over all the content. This book provides the necessary context to ensure that you get ALL the way to Fresh Start and not just in the front door.

It seems as if my whole life was leading up to this book, and my chance to transmute all that experiential capital of tears and pain into hope and love. It's been a long time in coming, but now I am able to make good on the promise to be that ray of sunlight for someone that made myself when I was thirteen. Good luck! And when you do get your Fresh Start, help me help the next person by following Gandhi's advice and being the change you wish to see in the world.

Cherie's Story

. . .

We weren't even thinking about moving. As a realtor I naturally watch as houses come and go from the market. One fall evening in 2006, I remember standing at the butcher's counter at Elverta Market, when I turned to my husband and said, " Hey, one of those houses in Cherry Creek came on the market today. You know those really cool ones on one-acre lots? Do you want to go see it?" It surprised me that I even asked the question, and it surprised me even more when he said, "Sure"! I quickly replied, "It's late, and I'm going out of town tomorrow. Let's forget it. Let's just go home and make dinner. "No, lets go!" he exclaimed. Intrigued by the enthusiasm stirring in us, we set out. It needed a lot of work, but it had tons of potential and was on a big beautiful lot. Our imaginations carried us away as we walked through the house and talked of all that could be done. The price tag was an irresistible $400,000. This exact house in the same condition would have easily sold for $500,000 only a year ago. It was a steal. Within hours, I was constructing an offer and sending it off, as I jumped on the plane to head out of town. Within two days, we were making our plans to move and gearing up for our dream "project." Using an interest-only loan with an adjustable rate, gave us an affordable payment, and no money down allowed us to sell our existing home and use the profit to remodel the new place. It was perfect. Let the adventure begin!

Fast-forward eighteen months, and we were having a very different conversation. It was about moving again, but this time it was about me moving out alone. With fourteen years of marriage almost unbelievably coming to a close, we had this house, this home, into which we had put all our money. Even in pristine condition, it was worth less than $300,000. We didn't have the $100,000+ difference between it's current value and the amount we owed, and neither one of us could afford the payment alone. I thought, "Okay. Stay calm. We've always paid on time, and we are excellent borrowers. I will contact our lenders and negotiate a loan modification. With my real estate background, it should be no problem, right?" Wrong. That reality was tough.

Months slipped by as we struggled to make two house payments and watched our savings dwindle at an alarming rate. We found ways to keep making the payments because we didn't want to "ruin" our credit, which we had worked so hard to achieve. With the evident hardship of a divorce, our lenders would surely help us while being current on the mortgage, right? Wrong again. Ouch.

More time slipped by and although I was successful at getting a modification on my second mortgage (while being current), it was evident that wasn't going to be the case with the first mortgage, and that was the one with which I really needed help. The truth was that we were out of savings and out of money. I took a long, deep breath and chose to stop making my payments.

It seemed unnatural, going against every fiber of my body, but what else could be done? I'd seen too many others who had used their retirement or racked up severe debt to hold on longer only for the inevitable to eventually happen. I was not going down that road. Why? Because by this point, I had at least figured out that my lender didn't have to help me and there was nothing I could do to make them. I didn't want to dig my hole any deeper than it was. What I wanted was to get out of the hole.

After many nights spent soul searching, we decided to put the house up for short sale. As hard as that was, it also was a huge weight lifted off my shoulders. No more wondering what am I going to do? Being in that place of uncertainty is simply exhausting. This relief didn't take away from the sadness that welled up every time I looked around at all the love and hard work that had gone into the home. I'll never forget the first call I received from someone to come see the house. I hung up and gently cried.

Acceptance is an amazing thing. It sets you free. Acceptance of all that is and was, allowed me to breathe in and breathe out, confident that everything was going to be okay because, well, it always was. Right? I mean we've all managed to get through everything in our lives up to this point. Why would this be any different? It wouldn't.

My journey through a divorce, a mortgage meltdown, and a short sale taught me two important things. First, I am not defined by a house, a credit score, or by the titles home owner or renter. I am greater than all those things combined. Each of us is a unique, beautiful human being that is defined by the kindness and love that we show in life. Second, I am not alone. We are all traveling through this human experience together. Experiencing the same things through different means. Who on this planet has not experienced pain, joy, loss, or love? In different ways, of course, yet still the same. We are more alike than different. Knowing that we all share these collective experiences is comforting because it means that we are never alone. This couldn't be truer when it comes to having a mortgage "challenge." There are millions (literally) going through it right now.

Around this same time I found myself in a conversation with my now close friend, Jesse. Knowing firsthand how it feels and how the system works (and how it's broken), the conversation went something like this:

"If it was THAT hard for me, I can only imagine the struggle for all those folks who don't know anything about the "inside." (I've been in real estate for ten years).

"I know," Jesse said. "The real estate community should be leading the healing."

There was a long silence, and then we started to speak at the same time.

"What about us?" I asked.

"What about a nonprofit?" Jesse replied.

Within weeks we were together in San Diego and Hope|against|HOPE, a nonprofit education and counseling organization, was born. Its sole purpose was to help the people in our communities. To shed light on all the mortgage chaos in a way that would give home owners the best chance of getting help and allowing them to make informed (not emotional) decisions regarding their housing situation. A year later, after presenting countless free workshops and giving away many Tool Kits at local libraries, we knew that it was working because of the continuous stream of grateful letters, e-mails, and comments from home owners. They all said something similar to "Thank you. I have hope, and I feel better. It's good to know that someone cares. Life still is good." We knew that there was no way we could keep this endeavor a secret and also knew that we couldn't possibly reach everyone who needed help. Our solution is this little book called Fresh Start.

The fact that you found it is no accident. It has a purpose and that purpose is to help you get your life back. Take what you need from this book, leave the rest, and start down the road to your Fresh Start today. Get your life back—you deserve it because it's the only one that you got.

Why Fresh Start as the Theme for my Next Best Step?

{5 Minutes}

· · ·

Lets start by defining Fresh Start: Resolution to the problem called distressed home owner by either staying the course, loan modification, short sale, or a mutually agreeable, mutually beneficial workout of any fashion with your lender(s). In the same way that a hardship is defined as anything negative that has happened since the inception of the loan that has contributed to your distress and subsequent inability to keep up your mortgage payments. Your Fresh Start exists on the exact opposite end of that spectrum.

You may know that there are stages of grief that people experience during difficult times. As you sit here, reading this, preparing to achieve your Fresh Start, it may help you to understand where you are now and where you're going next.

First there's shock: You're stunned and even frozen. Then comes denial. You can't believe it's happening to you. Then you feel <u>anger</u> at everyone and everything. Then comes bargaining, hoping that the bad news is reversible. Next is <u>depression</u>, seeing only a horrible end with nothing beyond it; this is followed by support, which is asking for help. The final stage is acceptance, when you're ready to move on to the next phase of your life. I wonder if you know where you're at right now?

Our goal for the investment of this time and energy must be two fold: feel better and fix the situation.

While we will get to the situation stuff once we start playing the game, let's check in with where we're at emotionally:

I am feeling _____

21) Ecstatic
20) Triumphant
19) Jubilant
18) Vivacious
17) Elated
16) Joyful
15) Happy
14) Pleased
13) Satisfied
12) Encouraged
11) Purposeful
10) Determined
9) Worried
8) Anxious
7) Frustrated
6) Angry
5) Discouraged
4) Disgusted
3) Depressed
2) Desperate
1) Miserable

I want to feel_____

What MUST you do next to start feeling better?

What Motivates You?

{5 Minutes}

. . .

Carrot & the Stick

One theme that has become clear over our years of helping people through change is that we are motivated by either moving toward budding pleasure or moving away from lurking pain. It just depends on how we are wired. Thankfully, both approaches work just fine. So, to ensure that we don't miss your buttons that could produce the impetus for some healthy change, let's look at the carrot versus the stick.

Carrot and stick is an old expression that refers to a policy of offering a combination of reward and punishment to induce behavior. Imagine a stubborn donkey hitched to your cart that just won't budge. In this case, the driver would tie a carrot on a string to a long stick and dangle it in front of the donkey, just out of its reach. As the donkey moved forward to get the carrot, it pulled the cart. Now imagine that same scenario, but after offering

the carrot just out of reach, the donkey still won't budge. I suppose it would only take a matter of exhausted patience to curse the poor result, untie the carrot, and regress to using the same stick against the donkey's rear end in a desperate attempt to achieve any result at all.

Now, we're not calling anyone donkey, but this is a great opportunity for us to spell out both sides of every coin. Considering both sides to every option allows you to make an educated decision about what your best options are at every stop along the way. So, what you will begin to notice is that at the end of each chapter, we will do our best to offer up both sides of the argument: for moving toward the direction of pleasure = ⸜ or away from the direction of pain = ⟋ . Here's to hoping you can find the utility in this.

Whether the carrot or the stick motivates you, allow one or both to lead you to your Fresh Start.

Meet Your Team

{10 Minutes}

• • •

"Hi. I'm Stewart Fresh. My friends call me LIL STEWEY. Okay, I've only got one friend, and he's invisible. I'll be your guide through this book and help you go from where you are to where you want to be. So, we're going to be friends. You'll see me pop up from time to time, break out my tool kit here, and offer my help. I'm kind of a big deal when it comes to helping out, and I hope you find this to be true for you.

Each step is like a landmark to your destination: Fresh Start. A step may be your final destination or an indicator that you need to move on to the next step. At the end of each step, you'll find the metaphor of the carrot and the stick empowering you by providing an impetus for change (toward pleasure or away from pain—whatever moves you forward).

At the end of this book, there are several short chapters that will assist in laying a foundation on which to build. Now, it's not important that you read all the chapters; what is important is that you find which ones are important for your particular situation and make it nonnegotiable that you at least ready yourself with them.

Okay, that's enough of me for now. Let's get started with the most important place to start in the entire book—Your Truth. I'll catch up with you a little bit later.

—LIL STEWEY

Meet Sarah: The Story Behind the Story

– Allow me to introduce Sara, the hero of this journey. She was the first person that we helped achieve a Fresh Start. She had been battling foreclosure and was ready to give up before we took inventory of where she had already been, and what she had already done. She had a great story; it was so inspiring that Cherie and I decided to immerse ourselves in her fight. She is a single mom with a single income working for a company doing what she loves. When her pay was suddenly cut by more than 20 percent, she was left with a home that was too big for her and her daughter, and a loan that she could no longer afford. She had bought the house with her ex-husband in 2005, and soon realized that it was already $100,000 upside down. She first tried to hire a loan modification company that required a $2,000 retainer fee. They kept her mostly in the dark for four to five months, feeding her tiny bits of what she called "useless information" before telling her there was nothing more they could do. They didn't charge her the rest of the $1,500 (total fee they agreed on was $3,500), but they kept the retainer fee. With a foreclosure date looming and no other options or hope, a friend introduced her to us. Over the next four months we helped her finally achieve what she was after. She agreed to share her invaluable lessons with you, in the form of the "Sara's Tips" in this book. So, you will notice that her tips are spread throughout (usually her sage advice and experiential wisdom **of what not to do** and what lesson she learned by doing it the wrong way, so that you won't have to repeat her mistakes).

So, it took all my energy, time, mistakes, etc to get to this resolution for my family. I careened from wall to wall, bruised and cut, clothes torn to arrive at clarity and my Fresh Start. It felt as if I had awakened on a deserted island, with limited food and water. A tattered treasure map washed ashore with an X marking where I was standing. I owed more than my house was worth and could no longer afford the payments. The map had an image of a treasure chest at the other end that represented my seemingly unattainable Fresh Start. There were lots of deadly pitfalls along the way. A perforated line that intermittently bridges these two things with points along the way that have curious names like loan modification, Obama Plan, bailout, hardship letter, and short

sale to name a few. But the distance was so unclear, the route so faded and the facts so shrouded in mystery that I felt alone and lost.

Furthermore, it felt as if the government and banks wanted everything unclear. I mean, if they really wanted to bail us out and retain us as the pivot to fix the economy, they would just make it simple, right? I'd get started on something and my bank would be bought by another bank. Then I had to wait for the new bank to take my note. Then the rules and process would be different. It was so frustrating! I had a treasure map I had found by piecing together scraps of information from the Internet. What I needed was clear, easy steps to take! I needed consistent, predictable, reliable advice that could take me, turn-by-turn, to my desired outcome. Letting me know what to expect and allowing me to prepare myself for each stage. I want to control my destiny and make the best decisions about the options I still have left. – Sarah

You've got your team. Now, we're not going to tell you that this book is every step you may or may not need to take because every situation is like a strange little snowflake. Who can walk into the blizzard of distressed home ownership with a microscope and identify the subtle nuances that separate one from the other? If that were true, we'd have to print one million unique editions of this book—one for each home owner. While that would be great, we don't need to because affecting positive change right now starts with a uniform approach to the solution.

This is a good time for two quick notes of housekeeping. The help available is timely and the legislature powering (funding) these programs have deadlines.

This information also has a shelf life. Meaning, what is true right now could change by the time it gets into your hands. It's true now…but there's no truth without context. And the only constant in this distressed home owner conversation is that everything is constantly changing. While we do our best to keep things as universally applicable as possible, be on the lookout for updated pieces supplementing the foundation we have established here.

The Following Pages Contain Your How, But What's Your Why?

{15 minutes}

. . .

It's been said, "You figure out your why, and God will figure out your how." That statement is more grounded in truth than religion. Zig Ziglar, perhaps the most famous motivational speaker and author of our time, has said, "You're either a wandering generality or a specific purpose." Starting anything with your why locked and loaded will be the catalyst that sees you through any endeavor.

Achieving your Fresh Start will prove to be no different. You'll need a strong enough why to get you through the how. Anything worth something will not and should not, come easily. The reason why people give up on their situation and leave with the unnecessary scars of a foreclosure on their permanent record is because they run into resistance. A single, "no", may send them packing. It may not seem so important to invest in defining your why when you just want to get going on the fix. And if that's your truth, I understand how you feel. I felt the same way when I started. But what was revealed to me is that there will come a time (it may come ten times) that I needed my why to get me through. So if not now, make sure you return to this exercise, so that when that time comes, you will be able to lean on it to stave off your resistance and keep you on track to accomplish your goal. Here is a simple exercise that can help you unveil your why:

It's called what's important to you about achieving this Fresh Start?

Our close friend, coach, and mentor Joe Stumpf introduced us to the idea that help always arrives as the higher truth in all we do. This will develop your clarity. Because with clarity comes vision. And someone much wiser than me once said, "You cannot achieve anything until you can visualize it happening first."

What's important about getting a Fresh Start to you?

_____

_____

_____

_____

What's important about (your above statement) to you? _____

_____

_____

_____

What would happen if you did get your Fresh Start?

_____

_____

_____

_____

What won't happen if you get your Fresh Start?

_____

_____

_____

_____

What won't happen if you don't get your Fresh Start?

_____

_____

_____

_____

Now its time to anchor it in when we put our signature to things, we are more likely to see them through so that we do not make a liar of the best parts of us. Take this moment to read, sign, date, and own this contract you are making with yourself to do what is necessary to see your Fresh Start through to the end.

My Contract with Myself

Right now I feel positive about my future. I have felt this way before. This time it will be different because I will create a workable plan of action and take each step. I will follow through completely with my commitment to myself and my future. By reading this book I have already taken the first step toward getting a Fresh Start in my life and feeling better.

Today I, _____, commit to getting my workable plan of action. I choose to create a better present and future for my family and I. I will do this by engaging my situation and doing whatever it takes, so that I can get on with life as I knew it.

I will not waver on my commitment to myself because I know what's important about getting this Fresh Start. Today I promise to do this.

Signed: _____
Dated: _____

Step One: Evaluate

{1 Hour}

. . .

The Cost of Staying the Course

As with any plan, especially one with many unknowns, a realistic assessment of your surroundings, what they mean and do not mean, and how it may affect each step to reach your destination is indispensable. The following exercises are such an assessment. Helping you to grasp exactly where you are right now and enabling you to make informed choices in the weeks and months ahead.

Example:
Prevalent Home Owner Situation Today

Owe: $280,000 on first Mortgage
$70,000 on second Mortgage
Total: $350,000

Current Value: $200,000 = $150,000 Upside Down
(Negative Equity)

Payment: $2,300
Renter next door pays: $1,300
Difference: -$1,000 every month

Recovery Time:
Let's imagine homes start
appreciating TODAY at 7 percent

Year 1:   214,000
Year 2:   228,980
Year 3:   244,923
Year 4:   262,067
Year 5:   280,041
Year 6:   299,643
Year 7:   320,061
Year 8:   342,465
Year 9:   366,437

Break Even: 8.5

Renter next door saved: $102,000
In actuality, one out of every six families is upside down
on its mortgage.

Now you try it:

- Owe First Mortgage: $_____
- Owe Second Mortgage: $_____
- What It's Worth Today: $_____

I Am + / — $_____ (equity)

Estimated appreciation per year: _____ % (Historically Housing = 5%)

Let's do the math:

$_____ X_____% _____ = $_____ Year 1

Today's value   Appreciation

_____ X _____ = _____ Year 2
_____ X _____ = _____ Year 3
_____ X _____ = _____ Year 4
_____ X _____ = _____ Year 5
_____ X _____ = _____ Year 6
_____ X _____ = _____ Year 7
_____ X _____ = _____ Year 8
_____ X _____ = _____ Year 9
_____ X _____ = _____ Year 10

Break Even Point: _____(months)

"Avoid problems, and you'll never be the one who overcame them." —Richard Bach

Realistic Financial Assessment

. . .

Now that you have surveyed your situation and understand where you stand with respect to the cost of staying the course (COSTC), it's time to take inventory of how much or little you have to work with during this journey. Armed with this knowledge, you will be prepared to enter negotiations along the way, confident that you know what is realistic for you and what is not.

Sarah's Tip

Remember the incidentals. Things like clothing (you can't go around naked after all…well you could but—yikes!), pet care, school supplies, recreation, and holidays (even if you are super thrifty you spend money then). Again the goal here is to get a true picture of what it costs for you to live in the real world.

Now let's get started…

Financial Worksheet

"Beware of little expenses; a small leak will sink a great ship"
—Benjamin Franklin

Where Do I Stand Right Now?

Monthly Expenses

Mort. 1st _____	Credit Card _____
Mort. 2nd _____	Utilities _____
Car _____	Food _____
Car _____	Cell/Internet _____
Insurance _____	Clothing _____
Gas/Parking _____	Recreation _____
Loans _____	Misc _____
Credit Card _____	Misc _____
Credit Card _____	Total Expenses _____

Total Monthly Income : _____

Total Income _____
minus
Expenses _____
= +/— $ _____

Each month I have a _____ of
$_____ **

** If you have high unsecured debt you may want to consider the option of bankruptcy as part of your Fresh Start plan. See section on Bankruptcy

If needed, I could cut my expenses in these areas:

1. _____
2. _____
3. _____

This would change my monthly residual by $_____

You now have a crystal clear view of your monthly supply versus demand. This means you are ready to enter into negotiations with your lender because you are clear about what you can really afford for housing.

Carrot

Awareness Theory – In 2005 the Braun Research Group reported that only about one-third of households use a budget (36.1 percent). Knowing that in any change attempt, 51 percent of the solution is just knowing and bringing the truth to light. Inviting the 500-pound gorilla in the room forward, defining it, and sprinkling some truth on it. When you do, you cut things out, put caps on others, and funnel more to what you want.

Stick

Studies suggest that the majority of families in bankruptcy were middle-class families with children who were pushed to insolvency by job losses, massive unexpected medical bills, or the devastating breakup of their families. These are educated folks, with all the protections in place, who just fell on tough times.

Financial distress is a lot like prison, and if you don't change your purpose, your friends, your skill set, and your environment, the things that got you into prison will send you right back. You'll end up stuck in the revolving door of financial dependence—even after your Fresh Start!

Finding Your Hardship

. . .

For your lender to work with you in any capacity, whether it is a loan modification request to preserve home ownership or a short sale to prevent foreclosure, one thing is almost always certain—you must show some type of financial hardship. Does it have to be an extreme hardship? Not necessarily. Do you have to show a deficit every month? Not necessarily. It just needs to be reasonable. What we are saying is that if you have a large surplus every month or a large amount in savings your lender may not be inclined to work with you.

Sarah's Tip

Don't worry: If you are having difficulty making your mortgage payments, then you have a hardship. If your savings is dwindling or your credit card debt is amassing then you have one too. Just ask yourself: What has changed in my life? There it is. That is your hardship. The next page will reveal the twelve most common hardships today. However, ANYTHING that has made it difficult or impossible to make your mortgage payments is a hardship. Find yours.

Your lender will require that you explain your situation in a hardship letter.

Sara's Tip: I learned two things in the process of submitting my first hardship letter to my lender. When the lender called me back and advised me that I needed to do it over, I learned to get off my high horse. With my second attempt, I did a little research on the art of letter writing. I learned about this technique psychologists use called grounding. Simply put this means that it's important to remember that a human being will read your letter. Even with all of our uniqueness and faults, human beings are all wired in the same way. We all have the same concerns, and they usually center in wealth, health, and relationships. Furthermore, we are most influenced by stories. So, the grounding technique is your ability to take the reader along on your story. Tell them what happened from the time you got the loan until now that has got you in this mess that needs fixing. It's important to know that they don't want an essay; it shouldn't be more than a page long. But in that page, get them invested in the story behind the story. Your financials will tell them the facts—the why.

"Every **hardship**, every joy, every temptation is a challenge of the spirit that the human soul may prove itself." —Elias A. Ford

Twelve Most Common Hardships

1. Mortgage Adjusts/Payment Increases
2. Loss of Job
3. Reduction in Income/Pay Cut
4. Business Failure
5. Death of Spouse or Family Member
6. Severe Illness/Medical Bills
7. Separation/Divorce
8. Relocation
9. Military Service
10. Excess Debt
11. Incarceration
12. Increase in Living Expenses (such as the birth of a child or caring for an elderly parent or grandchild)

The Actuality

It is estimated that most American families today could only maintain their current living expenses for sixty days or less when income is interrupted for any reason.

Sample Hardship Letter

Date: _____   (Grounding Technique)
Lender: _____   (Family Photo)
Attn: Loss Mitigation

RE: Hardship Letter—(Property Address)
Account Number

To Whom It May Concern:

I purchased my home in 2004, and we had the income at the time to support the mortgage. In early 2006, my mother was diagnosed with Alzheimer's disease and had to be put in a nursing home, which was very expensive. She passed away in November 2006, and my husband lost his job and has since taken a significant cut in pay. We love our home and do not want to lose it, but we have come to terms with the fact that we cannot afford to keep it.

This left me with the financial burden of paying the mortgage. I make $35,000 annually, and I have exhausted all of my savings, IRAs, and my children's college funds to keep the mortgage payments current until May 2007.

In May 2007, I was no longer able to make payments and inquired about partial payments, payment plans, and refinancing; I was denied on all accounts. In July 2007, I put the house up for sale.

My financial situation cannot sustain a home mortgage of nearly $2,800 a month. I want to sell the home, avoid foreclosure, and salvage my credit. I know that a foreclosure on my record will affect me for years to come, and I would ask that you please assist me in avoiding this. Since the house has been on the market, this is the only offer that we have received. Please accept this offer as payment in full. My realtor will continue to market the house, and if we receive any other offer they will be forwarded to you immediately.

I deeply appreciate your help and understanding in this matter. If you have any questions, or need anything further from me, please contact my agent or me personally.

Sincerely,

Hopeful Home Owner

The Two Part Conversation:

1. **Home ownership Preservation**
2. **Foreclosure Prevention**

• • •

To start, we are all taking the same steps in the same direction. At some point there is a fork in the road leading to the ultimate goal: a Fresh Start. Although both roads lead to the same destination, they take different steps. One road is called home ownership preservation. The other is foreclosure prevention. Let's start by defining these two roads.

Home ownership preservation:
Preserving your home ownership by making it affordable through a loan modification
or other workout.
Foreclosure prevention:
Avoiding the permanence of foreclosure through a short sale or deed in lieu.

We don't need to tell you that not everyone seeking to preserve their position as a home owner is able to because if you've looked at the statistics you already know that. What we would like to suggest is that in acknowledging that there are two possible roads leading to your Fresh Start, you have the best chance of succeeding. Leaving you equipped to make the needed adjustments and difficult choices that will come.

Carrot

Understanding your alternate route will lower your stress levels because you can be comforted by the fact that you already know what to do if you can't get the help you seek initially. It also gives you the highest assurance that you WILL avoid a foreclosure on your record come what may. If you get the help you need from your lender, that's Awesome. You can forget about the other road, happy in the knowledge that you were prepared but never had to take it. ☺

Stick

If you put all your eggs into one basket…well, do I even have to tell you what that means? You'll be left scrambling at a dead-end road if your lender doesn't give you the help you initially requested. Your option to take another route may be reduced or gone entirely because time has run out.

Pitfall:

· · ·

Short Term Fix versus Long-Term Solution

The short-term fix feels good. Yes, like stopping and stretching out on a hammock in the middle of a long journey. What is a short-term fix? Maybe a six-month forbearance or a new loan modification payment that you can't afford. The danger of the short-term fix is it feels so good that you can almost forget that you haven't reached your destination yet. It lulls you into a false sense of security. Sooner or later (in six or twenty-four months) you're going to have to get up. You'll be pushed out of that comfy hammock and back to that journey to get what you are ultimately after: a REAL solution. In the long-term only a permanent solution is going to give you the peace of mind that you deserve. Any experienced traveler would tell you to keep going. Because the effort it requires to get up and start again is monumental. The wisdom: have the focus and fortitude to go after the long-term solution so that your Fresh Start will truly be just that.

PITFALL:

Not figuring out how much help you need (monthly dollar amount)

Statistics show that nearly 50% of homeowners who receive a loan modification re-default. Why? The help was not enough.

Debe M. couldn't believe it. She didn't have enough to pay her mortgage again. How could this be happening when she was victorious in her loan modification process just four months ago? Her payments were lowered by $238 dollars a month! So why did it feel like she was living in the movie Groundhog Day? It wasn't until Debe sat down and did a honest, realistic financial assessment that the answer became clear. Although a victory, the $238 reduction simply wasn't enough. Looking at all her expenses, she would need a reduction of another $238 to make it work realistically. She realized she hadn't taken into account so many of the small expenses of life—things like toothpaste and toilet paper. This meant that Debe had to go to her lender to ask for help a second time. This time she made a promise that she shared with us: "I will be realistic and honest about what I can and cannot do. Even if I don't like it." She would not be traveling this road a third time.

Turn-by-Turn Instructions

. . .

1. Do the Cost of Staying the Course exercise. This will reveal the reality of your housing situation. You will be able to determine approximately how much negative equity you have and approximate how long it will likely take to recover to a break even point or positive equity situation. With this knowledge, you can choose whether your current situation is sustainable for the amount of time it will take to reach a positive equity position, or if you need (or just want) to seek help. If you choose to get help, then go to the next step.

2. Find your Hardship. Write a letter that gives your lender a "why" you need help.

3. Complete the Financial Assessment. Follow all the instructions and be both thorough and honest in this evaluation. This will help you determine: A) the other areas where you can make cutbacks, and B) how much you can realistically afford for housing. From this, you will see the discrepancy between what you are actually paying and what you can afford to pay. If you would like to stay in your home, then go to step

two. If you would like to leave your home, then go to step three.

"Money isn't the most important thing in life, but it's reasonably close to oxygen on the 'gotta have it' scale."
—Zig Ziglar

Step Two: Loan Modification

{1 Hour & 30 Minutes}

• • •

"Ninety percent of your work is the loan modification package. And forget any expectation you might have of a classic negotiation scenario in which you will get to fight it out over terms with a person because that won't happen. Your package does all the fighting.

Bonus: The work that you do here in step two, your Home Ownership Preservation Step, will be the same work that you do for step three, your Foreclosure Prevention Step. In the all-too-common event that a loan modification with your lender(s) is not reached."
—LIL STEWEY

We don't need to spend a lot time explaining what a loan modification is because by now you've probably figured that one out. A loan modification is when your existing mortgage company agrees to modify the terms of your existing loan. They fall into two categories: "in house" loan modification and Obama's MHA(Making Home Affordable) modification. What comes next isn't so easy to see.

What they aren't telling you:

...

Truth Number One
Not everyone is going to get a loan modification that will work for him or her.
Fair? No. True? Yes.

Truth Number Two
Despite truth number one, everyone should try.
If you can fog a mirror, and you have a loan, call your mortgage company and ask for help.

Truth Number Three
You don't have to pay someone to get a loan modification.
"Anyone who tells you differently is selling something"
—Princess Bride
In fact as of the date this was written, only about 20 percent of people who have a paid for that service have actually got one.

"The great enemy of the truth is very often not the lie—deliberate, contrived, and dishonest—but the myth—persistent, persuasive and unrealistic."
—John F. Kennedy

Loan Modification Secrets

. . .

Contact the number on your monthly mortgage state-ment or delinquent notice. Ask for loss mitigation/ loan modification contact information.

First call: Let them know who you are and give them your account number. After you get to the correct department, take great notes, always ask for names and write them down in a conversation log. Their process may or may not be to send you out a loan modification package with all their specific forms and disclosures to complete, sign, date, and send back; some lien holders will just give you a list of items needed and steps required that you have to write down. **Ask for the direct fax number to that persons department. Ask the person for estimated turn-around times and when to follow up next to confirm receipt of everything. Be specific—it adds creditability out of the gate. Call back at that exact time and keep calling until you get an update. (Don't be harassing, just punctual). **Goal of this call: To acquire ALL the information you need to submit your loan modification request, acquire the correct destination of those items (fax number, address, department, etc), and clearly gather the next steps. Remember it is important to know if you are applying for the HAMP program or an "in house" modification. The HAMP government loan**

modification program has very specific guidelines that you want to make sure you qualify for before applying for. (More information about this program later)

Second Call – Let the person know who you are, what you have already done, and that you are following up at the exact date/time as suggested. State that you have fullly disclosed & demonstrated your hardship and want to know if there are any specific required items or documents needed in order for this to get a priority decision. Request those items to be faxed over to you ASAP to reduce time wasted. **Goal of this call: To confirm that there is nothing more needed to process your request.**

Remember: ASK FOR TURN TIMES to be checked and the address to use if your materials are mailed or sent by FedEx. Ask for turn times on decisions. Keep great notes in your conversation log. We will tell you exactly how to put your package together in the next section.

Third Call – Follow up to confirm again that everything was properly received—all pages of each document—and that your file is complete (for now anyway). Ask for turn times on the decision. Keep great notes in your conversation log. **Goal of this call: Confirm what you thought you already knew, again. Don't rely on just one worker and just one phone call; you'll be amazed at how different the stories can be depending on who you get.**

Fourth Call – Follow up on the day the decision is supposed to be rendered if you have not been in contact before this time frame. If there isn't a decision yet, then build in a "time sensitive issue" for them to note in your file. Ground it in something real; stay away from make believe because if they call you on it (ask for documentation to support your claim), you better have it. Keep it within the parameters of your hardship; just tighten the screws to keep things moving and your file in the forefront of their minds. Every time you call ask if there are any missing documents or any documents that need to be updated. (They loose things often) Keep great notes in your conversation log. **Goal of this call: Make sure your package is still complete with no new requirements and if no decision has been made, build in time sensitivity to your situation.**

Fifth or More Call—Lather, Rinse, and Repeat :) (Same as above; keep the integrity high). It is suggested that you call at the very minimum every two weeks.

Putting Together Your Package

. . .

To give yourself the highest possible chance of success with a loan modification negotiation with your lender, your package will usually contain all of the following list. Remember before assembling your package call your lender and get a detailed list of their requirement and forms. (Step One in the Loan Modification Secrets)

Cover Letter

The cover letter should be clear, concise, and give the needed information to the bank. The information that you may want to include is a basic outline of what is included in your package, what you owe on the property, what it is really worth now, and mention the impending hardship. It's a good idea to write your name and loan number on all the documents in the package, so that if they get lost or misplaced, it will be easy to return them to the right file. Conclude your cover letter with all of your best contact information and state that you hope you can work together to resolve this issue.

Your Hardship Letter

Just make sure it's in there, feel comfortable referring back to the example if need be.

Financial Information

What the bank really wants to know is your inflow and outflow each month and what other obligations and assets you have. Usually this is done in the form of a financial worksheet such as the one you filled out during step one.

*In most cases the bank will request that the home owner complete the standard forms that they issue.

Supporting Financial Information

These items are typically the same as required when you were applying for a loan:

      Two years tax returns
      Two months pay stubs
      Two months bank statements

*It's important to note that for the bank to consider taking less than what is owed on the property, the owner needs to property, you need to provide the same type of information that you did when you applied for a loan, however now showing you can't do this financially at this time.

- ### Supporting Hardship Information

  If applicable. These are big! Don't omit them if they exist. For example, HOA (Home Owners Association) liens, medical statements, disability statements, divorce decree, bankruptcy paperwork, etc.

Comparables For Your Home to Determine Value

You definitely want to do your homework and pro-vide the bank with at least three to five comparables of properties in the area that have sold in the last nine months, preferably the last three months. In doing this, you want to try to get as close to your home as you can and ensure that you provide the most accurate (most like your home) comparables that you can. It might also be helpful to be able to show the number of days on the market and how many homes are currently for sale in your zip code. How do you get these?

> *Best: You can get these from a local real estate agent that you trust.
> *Next Best: Local title company will have access to recent sale activity.
> *Worst Case: Internet. It may not be reliable, but it's better than nothing—just make sure it's helping not hurting you.

County tax bill, HOA and Insurance information.

Be sure to include delinquent assessment amounts if there are any. Remember that if you are delinquent in any of these areas then the amount owing will increase on a daily basis. Include the county tax bill and verify any/all delinquent taxes that you know about.

Additional Information

Typically if a bank requires additional information, they will let you know what it is. The most common request that I have seen so far is for the payoff amounts from the other lien or mortgage holders on your property. The first mortgage holder may ask for a payoff amount from the second. You can get the payoff information by calling each lender and asking for it. Remember, the payoff amounts are time sensitive. Meaning if you are not paying your mortgage then each day that goes by your payoff would increase.

Conclusion

Your goal is to paint the most honest possible picture of your situation and to give accurate information about the local real estate market conditions that may or may not be contributing to your situation.

Not every bank is going to see the need to modify your loan as you see it, but if they don't accept on the first round, don't give up. Things change often, so keep all your hard work handy and try again in a short while to see if anything has improved that would allow them to reconsider you as a modification candidate.

Sarah's Tip

Here are my "3 truths" that I learned along the way:

Truth #1
Not everyone is going to get a loan modification that will work for them. Although I count myself as one of the "fortunate few" I have many a dear friends who were

not so fortunate. Once we collectively discovered this truth it somehow made it more palatable. Painful? Yes. Yet easier. It wasn't US it was the SYSTEM. Realization: despite the best of efforts sometimes things don't go as we would choose them to. This was a big Life Lesson for me.

Truth #2
Despite Truth #1 everyone should try. Looking back on this time in my life I wanted to rest in the knowledge that I did everything I could with what I had at the time.

Truth #3
You don't have to pay someone to get help. I'm living proof. I followed the advice given in this little book and got the help I needed on my own merit.

"If it's never worked before, try it just once more—that's what your heart is for." —J. Buffet

Making Home Affordable AKA: The HAMP Program

Obama's Program

• • •

In March 2009, President Obama announced the Making Home Affordable program. To date, it is the most successful of the government programs designed to help home owners. Since information is constantly changing, visit the official Web site to get the details on how it works and who qualifies.

For now we will give you the basics. The program is a federal program which means that it is nationwide. There are certain criteria that a homeowner must meet in order to qualify for the program. Here are the basics:

1. Borrower must be the principal resident of the home
2. Loan must be below $729,750
3. Loan must have been procured before January 1, 2009
4. Homeowner must have a financial hardship

For more information, visit http://www.makinghomeaffordable.gov.

The guidelines for this program are very specific. Know what they are before you start so that you don't waste precious time if it's not the program for you. If it represents your best choice—perfect. If not, keep moving down the road to your next best option.

Carrot

All of the obstacles and considerations at this point may make the steps to getting your Fresh Start seem overwhelming. Stay focused on the destination ahead—your Fresh Start. Imagine staying in your home at a payment you can afford. How good would that feel?

Stick

Lets say it's ten years from now. It's a cool Saturday morning, and you're mowing the lawn. Your friendly neighbor sparks up a conversation about stuff, and the conversation somehow slips into money. You don't usually talk about that topic with him, but it continues. He proceeds to share that they're getting ready to sell their home and what they are going to do with the proceeds. Shocked by the number, you remember that you both bought about the same time. You probe and he gushes, "Oh yeah, well about ten years ago, when that whole housing crash happened, Mary and I were able to negotiate down that payment to about half of what it was then. We got through it because of that and when Mary got her job back from the county, we started putting almost her whole paycheck toward the mortgage. Do that for as long as we did, and that thing goes down fast." While you want to be happy, what pulverizes you is the fact that you and your neighbor work at the same job and make about the same salary! Your spouse doesn't work either! Just "because you could get by, you didn't even try." Now, they are ready to close this chapter of their life and start living their dreams of retirement, and you are still stuck with your big house payment. Now imagine that scenario with its unfortunate ending and now check in with me on your "pride of ownership." It's the same yard, it's the same front door, and it's the same house payment—let's just see if we can't let you keep a little more.

Pitfalls

• • •

Not realizing that your second lien holder makes ALL the difference

The second mortgage: the less obvious monthly burden. One of the big takeaways in the financial assessment is that everything counts. That's right from cutting Starbucks to asking your second lien holder for help. Imagine your payment going from $369 to $218. Our bet is you could find a better way to spend that $151 bucks a month than give it away in interest to your lender. The best route is to engage in a conversation with all of your lien holders about how they can collectively help you.

Relying on an older, basic fax machine to get the job done.

These incoming fax machines that your lender is using are handling unrealistic volume. The only way your fax is going to make it there is if you have one of those newer, fancy fax machines with the automatic feeder that takes the whole fax and sends it as one file. The cheaper, older models that transmit one page at a time probably aren't going to cut it. You may want to spend the money and go to Kinko's or a local copy store and use their fax instead. Regardless of what kind of machine you use, ALWAYS request a "fax confirmation sheet" to ensure it went through. Another option is to overnight the package to your lender.

They said they would call…..

"But they said they'd call!" Sounds like a flimsy promise made over a first date that didn't go so well. Unlike that scenario, when dealing with your lender, it is imperative that you make the first move and the second and the third…you get the drift. No matter what promises your lender makes ("Hey, we'll call you"), make your own promise to yourself to call and follow up as many times as it takes because your LIFE depends on it.

Question Everything. (Politely, of course.)

Much like this planet, this journey to your Fresh Start is a living, breathing entity. The rules and the people who facilitate those rules are constantly changing and evolving. This is so true that the opportunity for misinformation, miscommunication, or just plain mistakes is significant. Chances are along the way someone who picks up the line down at your lender's loss mitigation department is going to get something wrong. Intentionally? Probably not. Yet, the potential impact of this to your Fresh Start could be devastating. So, if it doesn't seem right, heck even if it does, ask again. Call, talk to a different representative, ask the same questions, and maybe a few new questions. Fearlessly (and kindly) question EVERYTHING.

Misjudging your odds (or worse not knowing them at all). Would you bet in Vegas without them? Why bet your Fresh Start without knowing them.

Statistics reveal that approximately 10% of homeowners with negative equity have successfully received a loan modification.

Being realistic about your odds of getting the help you seek is important because it gives you the insight and ability to navigate the steps to your fresh start with the highest likelihood of success. You need not look further than the above statistic to know that not everyone asking for help is getting it. Know your odds, so that you can plan accordingly. We've seen one too many home owners with low odds on getting a loan modification in the first place end up with no time left and a foreclosure at their doorstep. Don't let this be you. Plan ahead.

Turn-by-Turn Instructions

・ ・ ・

1. Call your lender(s) and ask what loan modification programs they offer. If they offer the Making Home Affordable program, determine if you meet the basic guidelines. If you do, then ask how to apply for the program. If not, ask what in-house modification programs they offer and how to apply for them.

2. Follow your lenders' instructions exactly. **Only submit your package if it is complete**. Once you've submitted, follow up in forty-eight to seventy-two hours to verify that all pages were received. (Refer to the LM secrets section)

3. Call your lender every ten to fourteen days to follow up. Always ask if they have ALL documentation needed. (They lose things quite often.) Keep a detailed conversation log. If you get an unhelpful or unfriendly representative, simply hang up and call back.

4. The review process generally takes sixty to one hundred and eight days.

5. If your lender denies your request, ask why and determine if you can change any of the factors such as increasing your income if it was deemed too low. If not, ask if there are any other programs for which you can apply. If so, repeat steps one through four and apply for the alternate program. If not, ask

yourself whether you can stay the course. If not, go
to step three.

6. If your lender gives you a loan modification offer,
review it carefully and compare it with your financial assessment. Ask yourself if it is realistic considering your current finances? If it is, make sure all
terms are agreeable. Check how long the terms
run and how they will change over the years. Sign,
return the modification, and begin your Fresh Start.
If the terms of the loan modification are not realistic with your current financial situation, ask your
lender if there are any other programs for which
you can apply. If so, repeat steps one through four
and apply for the alternate program. If there are no
alternate programs, ask yourself if it is possible to
stay the course without a reasonable modification.
If not, go to step three.

Step Three: Short Sale

{1 Hour & 30 Minutes}

• • •

So, What Is a Short Sale?

A short sale is when your lender agrees to allow your home to be sold by accepting less then the amount owed against the home because there is not enough equity to sell now. For example, a seller might have a loan balance of $300,000 and a buyer that is willing to pay only $150,000. If the lender accepts the offer, he has agreed to "short sale" the amount owed by $150,000. This means your lender takes the loss—not you. Because not all lenders will negotiate a short sale, and because a short sale involves complex paperwork, a well-qualified real estate agent is key.

You can't just wake up one morning and decide you're going to sell your home at a loss by asking your lender for a short sale. Sometimes, lenders won't even consider a short sale if your payments are current. If your payments are behind, lenders are often more agreeable to a short sale. Also, if you have cash assets, the lender might try to tap those accounts. I guess what we are saying is that there are various aspects to consider when doing a short sale. With that said for many a short sale is the best remaining option.

Why Would a Lender Accept a Payoff for Less than the Loan Amount?

As you have probably heard, many lenders are taking large losses. They must manage and mitigate these losses. The truth is the short sale option can be a good alternative to foreclosure. Sometimes it can be financially advantageous for your lender to accept a payoff for less than the loan amount, rather than foreclose on the property. (The average cost of a foreclosure to a bank is $60,000!) Of course, there must be a willingness on the lender's side to negotiate a short sale for it to work.

3. Who and What Situation Qualifies for a Short Sale?

The main requirement is proof of hardship, just as in a loan modification scenario. All the hardships listed earlier would apply here. If your lender has denied you a loan modification, they will have a record of this, and it may influence them to approve you for a short sale workout.

What Are the Costs?

Intended

Traditional Sale Costs:
Commissions—Real Estate
Title/Escrow
Transfer Taxes—utilities, taxes.

In most cases, your lender will agree to pay for all of the costs associated with the sale. This means zero out of your pocket.

Unintended

Possible Tax Consequences:
Historically if you sold a home short, the difference was considered debt forgiveness and was taxed as income to you. Ouch! The good news is that on December 20, 2007, the Mortgage Debt Forgiveness Act was passed. This exempts many home owners from any tax liability. This is HUGE! It's kind of like a get out of jail free card. Consult a qualified tax professional to find out if you qualify.

How Does It Work?

Step One: Interview and find a realtor experienced with short sales. Remember, you want the person working for you to have the ability and expertise to get it done. Use the Real Estate Agent Cheat Sheet.

Step Two: List the home for sale.

Step Three: Receive an offer, and negotiate best terms possible.

Step Four: Thirty to one hundred twenty days for the short sale approval process. (Agent oversees all these details.)

Step Five: Receive approval. Begin escrow. Close in thirty days or less.

Step Six: Move and begin the next chapter of your life. :-)

Home Affordable Foreclosure Alternative AKA: HAFA Program

President Obama's Extended Plan

. . .

The Obama Administration announced incentives and uniform procedures for short sales under its new Foreclosure Alternative Program (FAP). For borrowers who are unable to retain their home under the Making Home Affordable Loan Modification Program, lenders may consider a short sale or, if that is not successful, a deed-in-lieu of foreclosure.

This program is a huge "win" for homeowners that did not receive a loan modification and are now looking for a graceful exit. It allows them to avoid the permanence of a foreclosure and get a fresh start. The big benefits of the HAFA program are that homeowners receive $3,000 towards moving costs and are released of all liability on the loan.

For all the information on this program visit the official website at:

http://makinghomeaffordable.gov/hafa.html

Real Estate Agent
Interview Cheat Sheet

. . .

What's more important than knowing all the complex workings of how the short sale process works? Choosing WHO helps you. Here's why:

National Average of Successful Short Sales:
< 20 percent

If you were in Vegas, would you bet on those odds?
Statistics show that experienced short-sale real estate agents have a success rate close to 80 percent. While that's no guarantee, it's drastically better odds.
Since the whole goal here is avoiding the permanence of having a foreclosure on your record, it is imperative that you have the right agent on the job. Here's your cheat sheet to make sure it happens:

1. Have you ever done a short sale? How many short sales have you closed?
2. What lenders have you worked with thus far?
3. Do you have any accreditations in this specialization?
4. (If you have two loans.) Do you have any experience managing junior lien holders?

4.5 Will you be doing own negotiations? (Tip: Be wary if they use a third party to negotiate for them; in that case, they are giving the responsibility to someone else. Out of sight, out of mind.)

CPA/Tax Accountant Interview Cheat Sheet

• • •

One of the BIG benefits of a short sale is the Mortgage Debt Forgiveness Act of 2007, which gives many home owners a complete exemption from tax liability. It is imperative that you meet with a knowledgeable tax accountant to determine your eligibility for an exemption from mortgage debt forgiveness tax. If you do not qualify, you may be able to declare insolvency. A good certified public accountant (CPA) is an indispensable guide for you. Here is your cheat sheet to make sure you select an accountant that has the experience needed in this special area.

1. Are you familiar with how the Mortgage Debt Forgiveness Act works?
2. How will our state tax laws affect me? How will federal laws affect me?
3. Can you tell me how the insolvency exemption works?
4. In your experience, how will the loss mitigation of doing a short sale affect my overall financial health (specific to their expertise of course) moving forward, versus a foreclosure?
5. What things have you seen people do wrong, what mistakes have you made, or seen made

when working within the tax strategy of someone who has done a short sale?

Sarah's Tip:

At one point someone told me to just walk away. I'll admit that the idea was as tempting as a Siren's call. Although I loved my home and cared about my credit, I was emotionally, mentally, and even spiritually exhausted. How much longer could I keep going? On the brink of exhaustion, I discovered the truth about walking away—it just isn't possible. All the consequences such as tax implications remain and in fact, are exacerbated because of the increased costs that the bank would push on me. They don't walk away just because you do. This sobering reality gave me the energy to keep going. My future and credibility depended on it.

Deficiency Judgments*

• • •

Definition: An assessment of personal liability against a mortgagor, a person who pledges title to property to secure a debt, for the unpaid balance of the mortgage debt when the proceeds of a foreclosure sale are insufficient to satisfy the debt.

In some cases your lender may pursue a deficiency judgment against you for the loss they incurred. Yes, that's right. In some cases, they can try to come after you personally after the fact. There are many factors that determine if you are at risk of a deficiency judgment from your lender. It depends on your particular state laws, the type of mortgage you have (recourse or nonrecourse) and a host of other factors. Rather than write a fifty-two-page dialogue (one for each state), we are just going to cut to the chase:

If you are faced with foreclosure, you need to speak with a local expert that is familiar with your state laws and can advise you regarding your situation. An expert will also be able to advise you regarding your options if your lender does seek a deficiency judgment.

Remember the possibility of a deficiency judgment is present with foreclosure, deed-in-lieu, or a short sale. If you lender is taking a loss on the property, they may (or may not) be able to come after you for the difference. Be prepared and know not only your risk but also your rights. It is suggested to consult an attorney for this.

Help May Be on The Way

The government short sale program, Home Affordable Foreclosure Alternative (HAFA), provides relief for homeowners. Lenders who approve a HAFA short sale for a homeowner also waive the right to pursue a deficiency judgment. This is a big victory for homeowners. Some states are also helping out such as California. As of July 2011 a law was passed (SB 458) which states that for a limited time if homeowners do a short sale in California their lender cannot pursue a deficiency judgment. The passing of SB458 is a move in the right direction. It is our hopes that other states will follow suit and starting helping homeowners move on to a fresh start.

Pitfalls

. . .

We're not encouraging you to play realtor here because that role is for the professionals you have carefully selected. But wouldn't it be empowering to know just a few of the big deal killers so you can protect yourself in the process? You betcha. Take the following to heart because with a national close average of 10-20 percent at the time of this writing, there is obviously a lot that can, and may go wrong.

I Can't Afford to Do a Short Sale.

Maya A. looked at me and said, "Listen, I can't even pay my mortgage. How do you expect me to pay the costs associated with selling my home?" Listening to Maya, I realized that she was not alone. Many, maybe even most, of the home owners out there were asking the same question. It's important that Maya and every home owner understand that in almost all cases your lender will agree to pay the entire cost of the sale. That could mean no out-of-pocket expenses for you.

"How could THAT be?" Maya quickly asked. It all comes down to dollars and sense. Foreclosure is very expensive business. The truth is foreclosure costs your lender thousands of dollars. Your lender has one overarching goal—to minimize or mitigate their losses. They do this by agreeing to pay for the costs associated with the short sale. Were talking real estate commissions, title, escrow—the whole caboodle. It costs more in both time and money to carry out a foreclosure. I can't tell you how many folks have fallen into the sand trap of foreclosure because they thought they couldn't afford a short sale workout.

Maya completed her short sale ten months ago, and today she says, "I'm almost halfway into my rebuilding process, and I'm looking forward to becoming a home owner again sooner rather than later thanks to the fact that I was able to do a short sale with zero cost."*

* Of course what your lender will agree to pay for is strictly at their discretion.

Making sure the offer is reasonable

Make sure that the offer represents market value. Market value here refers to the evidence that supports the estimated value of your home today. This is an arbitrary number, most closely reflected by the most recent sales activity in your neighborhood, from like properties. Simply put, if you own a 1,500-square foot, three-bedroom, two-bath home with a garage, what have similar homes sold for over the course of the last ninety days or so. The number one, foolproof way to get your short sale denied is to present them an offer that they feel is too low; that would make it less expensive to just foreclose on you and try their hand at selling your house for more. There's no magic number here; this is part of the skill of the seasoned short sale expert, so choose wisely. And before you send that offer over to your bank for their approval, huddle up with your agent on the figure and ask for the recent comparables that support or disprove the suggested number before your lender disproves them for both of you.

The highest offer is always best. Or is it?

The highest offer isn't always the best offer. After securing an offer that you mutually deem represents market, the next mistake is when agents forget that their old market hat is on and fail at the selection process. This is understandable because the old market had different rules and different practices. In this new marketplace, the secondary concern (once market value is attained) is to choose a buyer and buyer's agent that give you the best chance of closing. Allow me to explain. In the last market, if you got five offers on your property, you leaned toward the highest offer, assuming that the buyers were qualified to borrow the required amount and could prove that they had the funds and ability to close on time. You could argue that this would apply to any market, and you wouldn't be wrong. Indeed, it is still in your (and your lender's) best interest to secure the highest price someone is willing to pay. This minimizes your potential financial obligation to the bank and, in doing so, increases the chances the bank will approve the transaction (see pitfall number one). So where's the pitfall? You have to look further into the unknown to truly grasp why it's imperative that your selection process is your primary concern.

a. Appraised Value – Remember, no matter what you accept, if the buyer is securing financing to acquire the property, an appraiser has to find proof that the home is worth at least that much, or there's no deal.

b. All-Cash Offer – No loan? You hit the jackpot, right? Maybe. All-cash offers have a tendency to feel as if the entire market owes them something and are typically the most transient by nature. In a declining market, the chances of the buyer for your home finding a better deal and walking from the commitment made to you before you receive short sale approval from your bank, seems to be highest with the all-cash buyers.

c. Pricing Ahead of the Market – Don't take the buyers word for it! They are just trying to get their offer accepted before the competition does. Even if you chose a strong buyer and submitted the offer to your bank for approval, along with plenty of support for that number, it doesn't mean it will hold that value. It is not un-common for short sale approvals to take three to six months or more, especially when you have more than one lender. The comparable sales in the neighborhood may have supported a price point of $300,000 in March, but are looking more like $275,000 going into October. If your buyer walks and pursues a better deal, you may be relegated to start the entire short sale process over again, which could throw you into foreclosure if you can't plead with your bank to grant you more time.

Coming up Short: The Second Lien Holder

There is a dance that no one talks about all that much. Maybe that's because it's not a gay, happy dance you might see in the movies. It's a silent dance that takes place between your first and second lien holder at the coaxing of your realtor. The well-intentioned outcome of this dance is for both parties to part ways willingly and satisfied, that is, both lien holders agreeing to a said payment and approving the short sale. Every now and again it doesn't end quite this civilly. Neither lender is willing to take what the other is willing to give—an impasse. How do you ensure that this impasse doesn't leave you hanging with a foreclosure? During the months of the short sale approval process, start putting money away in a fund to ensure you get your Fresh Start. Chances are your lenders will acquiesce if you bring in the difference. In many cases the amount needed is less than $5,000.

Backup Offers Are GOLD

Stephanie was thrilled to be getting the keys to her new home. It felt a little like a dream because her offer had been the third backup offer in line. It had seemed like a long shot at best. But here she was getting her keys because the three buyers before her had all disappeared. During the months of waiting they had moved on. That was okay with her, she thought, as she smiled and walked through the door of her new place.

Be careful about believing that one offer is enough or that one buyer will wait until the end. Experience shows that it's usually the second or third buyer in line that will actually buy your home. Why? Because waiting is hard to do, and buyers can be lured away by other homes that are out there. Homes with a shorter wait time. Imagine getting your short sale approval with no buyer around to complete the sale. The savvy seller knows this and continues to market their property while going through the process because backup offers are gold.

Communication Is Crucial

Okay now that you have that sought-after buyer and maybe even a golden backup offer or two how do you increase your chances at getting them to stick around? Communication. Keep them party to the progress, give them weekly updates and be their emotional cheerleader. Ensure you use comments like "We are getting closer, and we are working hard to make this happen for you."

If you let weeks—dare I say months—go by without talking to the prospective buyer then he or she will think, "Nothing is happening, and there's no forward progress. Maybe I should start looking elsewhere." Communication is crucial and will help keep your buyer(s) in place

Unknown, Forgotten, and Remembered Liens against the Property.

Dangerous Pitfalls: Mechanics liens, child support liens, IRS liens, and anything similar. These liens must be released from the property in order for your short sale workout to happen. The good news is that it generally can be done, and your trained real estate agent can guide you through the process. Starting early is key. If you know or even suspect a possible lien, tell your real estate agent about it immediately. The agent can have a title search done that will determine if the lien is attached to the property or not. If the existence of liens comes as a nasty surprise at the very end of the sale process, there might not be the time to resolve it and salvage the sale. You could lose out on your Fresh Start. I remember how Seth, a home owner is California, was astonished when a lien appeared on the title report. Then the vague memory of that dispute with the yellow pages started to resurface from the recesses of his mind. "Yes, that's right," he said, "I told them to cancel the ad, and they didn't. They said I never cancelled, and I refused to pay them the $3,200. I kind of forgot about it." Out of sight, out of mind- for a time anyway. The lucky news for Seth was that his real estate agent was shrewd enough to catch it early. He was thrilled to hear that they would agree to lift the lien for a payment of $500. Now he was getting two Fresh Starts—the big one with his house workout and the smaller one with this old skeleton in the closet gone for good

HOA Dues: The Silent Killer

Ron P. was thrown into confusion when he got a letter from his home owners association that they were starting foreclosure proceedings! What? "Can they even do that?" he asked? "Yes," I confirmed. "They can, and they will." (This is possible in many states.) Like, Ron, if you become delinquent on your HOA dues they DO have the right to foreclose. Yep. Avoid this pitfall, by checking your state laws. Know if and when your HOA can foreclose on your property. It's interesting to note that lenders often don't include past due HOA fees in their settlement agreements, and some HOAs have first right of refusal, which can derail a smooth transaction.

Find out if you have PMI

Many lenders today are putting private PMI on properties. PMI stands for Private Mortgage Insurance. The
quick definition is that it is an insurance policy that
protects the lender in the event that the homeowner
defaults on the loan. If you have PMI it will effect your
short sale process. There's not anything you can do
about it. You just want to know what you're dealing
with. Have your real estate agent find out.

Turn-by-Turn Instructions

. . .

1. Meet with a qualified CPA to determine if you will have any tax consequences.
2. Meet with a real estate attorney to find out if you will have any other risks or legal considerations that may be associated with doing a short sale.
3. Review the real estate cheat sheet. Interview and find a real estate agent that specializes in short sales.
4. Have your real estate agent help you to determine if you may qualify for a HAFA short sale.
5. Provide all financial data to your real estate agent.
6. Put the home on the market.
7. Market and show property until you receive an offer at the current market value.
8. Your real estate agent will submit the offer and financial package to your lender(s).
9. The review process takes from thirty to one hundred and twenty days. If your lender denies the short sale request, go to step four. If your lender approves the short sale you will begin the traditional thirty-day escrow period.
10. The buyer will complete inspections/appraisals. Sign final closing papers and close escrow. Begin your Fresh Start.

Step Four: Bankruptcy, Deed-in-Lieu, and Foreclosure

{35 minutes}

• • •

What about Bankruptcy?

Don't make the mistake of thinking about bankruptcy as an island! If you're leaning in that direction, you need to weave it into the plan of what to do with your home. It can limit or enhance your options, so get good advice first! The reason for this: Bankruptcy is a BIG gray area. Who should, who shouldn't, when, and when not? It's a weighty matter to consider because of the long-term shadow a bankruptcy will cast on your credit. When do the pros outweigh the cons? Every family's situation is unique and because of this fact, professional leadership is crucial. If you're even thinking of bankruptcy, the advice you get and choose to follow will affect your life for a long, long time. Bankruptcy, like foreclosure, is a permanent strategy and will play a role in all the preceding options in this book.

Sarah's Tip:

Yep, I just picked up the yellow pages, thumbed through, and found the attorney with the biggest ad. Sitting there in that office one Monday afternoon, the notion that I might have other options was quickly swept out the door, and bankruptcy was presented as the only viable option for me. Instead of feeling confident because of my understanding of my options, I just felt like no one was listening.

The second time around I found an attorney who was referred to me by someone I respected. Leaving that attorney's office, I had clarity about how each decision would affect me positively and negatively. I did have a choice. It was a tough one, but it was a choice. Experience showed me that when you're dealing with something as big as bankruptcy, make sure you're talking with someone you can trust and who has your best long-term interests at heart.

What about a Deed-in-Lieu?

. . .

What is a Deed-in-Lieu (DIL)?*

The U.S. Department of Housing and Urban Development defines it as: "A Deed-in-Lieu of foreclosure (DIL) is a disposition option in which a mortgagor voluntarily deeds collateral property in exchange for a release from all obligations under the mortgage." An easy way to think of it is as a "voluntary" foreclosure. You sign back the property to the lender, and they don't have to go through the legal proceeding of a foreclosure.

Are There Advantages to a DIL?*

The primary advantage is that a DIL looks better on a home owners credit report than a full foreclosure. However, it should be noted that the DIL is only one step better than the foreclosure, so it will not do much to improve the credit score. Its main benefit will be to prevent the worst of the credit damage that foreclosure can cause.

The DIL is usually not the best option to stop foreclosure; the truth is that it does not do a whole lot to improve the home owner's credit. Its main benefit is as a last-ditch effort to prevent the damage of foreclosure to your credit when no other options are available. It also ends the whole process sooner and results in fewer derogatory notifications against the credit profile, otherwise, known as "mortgage lates" However, if selling the property or a short sale can be done, these solutions can often present much better results for the long-term financial health of the home owner than a DIL of foreclosure.

What if I have two mortgages?

You probably cannot get a DIL if you have second or third mortgages, home equity loans, or tax liens against your property. Why? Most lenders will not agree to accept a deed-in-lieu of foreclosure when there are two loans on the same property simply because the junior liens are not wiped out in such a case. That is, if the first mortgage lender accepts a DIL, he'll have to take over the property and the junior liens. As such, the property doesn't have clear title. Lenders will almost always either opt for a short sale because the second lien holder signs off in this scenario or a foreclosure where the second lien holder is wiped out by the proceedings.

* Note: With the deed-in-lieu or foreclosure option, you would want to meet with a qualified CPA and real estate attorney to determine the legal and tax consequences.

The Reality of Foreclosure*

(NOT sugar coated)

. . .

You did everything you could to stay the course. Multiple loan modification requests were denied. You exhausted the short sale process to the very end. Even then, you kept going. Nothing. Your lender can and will foreclose despite all your effort. Sometimes in the game of life you can't win for trying. There may be nothing more you can do because you've already done it.

"Then you will know the truth and the truth shall set you free" —John 8:32

Set yourself free in the knowledge that you did EVERTHING you could with what you had. You played the game till the finish line, and when you look back in one, ten, or twenty years, you can be at peace because you did all that could with what you had. And that's all we can do in this game called life, is it not?

Don't let yesterday take up too much of today. "The future is always beginning now." —Mark Strand

* Note: With the deed-in-lieu or foreclosure option, you would want to meet with a qualified CPA and real estate attorney to determine the legal and tax consequences.

Turn-by-Turn Instructions

• • •

1. If you have high unsecured debt or the possibility of a large deficiency judgment you may want to consider bankruptcy as part of your Fresh Start. If so, meet with an attorney (preferably one found through referrals) who can help you determine the possible advantages of this choice.

2. If your lender has denied your loan modification and/or short sale request, ask about the option of a deed-in-lieu. If you lender will allow it, follow their instructions and complete the deed-in-lieu. Working within their time frame, you will be able to plan your move and begin your Fresh Start. If they will not allow a DIL go to step three.*

3. In some cases foreclosure is the only option left. (Please note that in some cases foreclosure is the best option specifically for investors. Consult a real estate attorney to find out.) If this is the case, call your lender and attempt to find out where you are in the foreclosure process. Also, ask how long they project it will take to complete the foreclosure. Chances are they will not be able to give you exact dates, however you may be able to get a rough estimate. Start looking for a new place, move, and begin your Fresh Start.*

* Note: With the deed-in-lieu or foreclosure option, you would want to meet with a qualified CPA and real estate attorney to determine the legal and tax consequences.

What the (_____) Happened?
(The Abridged Version)

· · ·

What we are not going to do is rehash. There will be no talk of the housing market or Wall Street. But, spending a paragraph on what happened can be helpful because it gives us the chance to start from the same spot. And in doing so, unite our collective voice while ridding us of the shame that can sometimes accompany the distressed home owner. The best way we can do this is with a quick story:

There was this couple, right here in California, who bought at the tippy-top of the market about three years ago. After surveying their many financing options, they decided to go with a five-year adjustable rate mortgage ARM that was sure to implode at the sixty-first month if they didn't refinance by that time. Well, you know how this story unfolds…the husband was in the construction industry, and the wife a real estate agent. The marriage dissolved, and the home was 20 percent upside down. They needed to sell immediately!

As you can imagine, this couple was in a world of hurt, and I know because I am referring to my story. Now, you might say, "Cherie, how could you let that happen? You are a real estate agent. Didn't you know better? And the truth is that, we were all addicted to "hope-ium"! Most of us thought that in five years time we would be another $50,000 richer, and we'd be sitting back formulating our next move. Perhaps we'd sell at a profit and buy into that neighborhood that had been just out of our reach. Well, it just didn't work out that way. And like 50 percent of my neighbors, we found ourselves needing help and there was little or none to be found. At the time of this writing, we've catapulted from a typical foreclosure rate of 1-4 percent to 12-14 percent, which is the highest ever since that figure has been tracked.

My motivation for that level of disclosure is clear: What I aim to do is to eradicate the shame that keeps the distressed home owner silent and stationary while dispelling the myths that foreclosure prevention is an us versus them conversation. The truth is that even if this story doesn't resonate with you at all, we are still all in this together. Because what I do with my home directly affects the value of your home. In fact, the White House released a sobering statistic in early 2009 that we have come to call the 9 percent rule: Every time a new foreclosure enters a neighborhood, it immediately drops the values of all the homes in that neighborhood by 9 percent. So you can see, it's vital that we choose to check our damaged and bruised ego's at the door, choose to stop participating silence and shame of this growing problem, and choose to be part of the solution.

.

Survival and Replication

. . .

The ultimate purpose in life is survival. The penultimate purpose in life is replication (nature's long-established engine of survival).

Okay, Darwin, what does this have to do with a distressed home owner?

Bound by the human condition, you have a hierarchy of needs and everything you do results directly or indirectly from emotions that demand you and your family meet them. What could be truer than the very real possibility that our safety, which according to the famous psychologist Abraham Maslow is our second highest hierarchy of needs, is in jeopardy? In fact, being a distressed home owner is a two-pronged attack on our safety because it doesn't just threaten our shelter—it threatens to negate our financial well being in one fell swoop! Throw in an innocent victim or three (significant other and kids), and now you don't only have safety concerns, you've got yourself some survival and replication concerns.

Certain lower needs must be satisfied before higher needs can be met. Think about it, if you were drowning in a pool, your need for oxygen would supersede your need for love. If nobody loved you, it would stink, but you wouldn't die instantly. Safety establishes stability and consistency in a chaotic world. The rest of the chart shows that without safety none of the higher needs can live or be sustained.

Opinion Alert: this could contribute to our high divorce rate. Most divorces are attributed to money concerns (safety). As a matter of fact men, women are more interested in your stability (survival) than your looks (replication)! From an evolutionary perspective, if these lower needs weren't met, it would mean death.

With our perceived mental and financial well-being dependent on our safety, and our financial well-being dependent on our credit, and our credit dependent on how bad this distressed home owner thing gets, it's no wonder that we are processing a lot of fear and anxiety right now. That is because the outcome could mean our ability to survive and replicate!

A little homage to our friend fear

• • •

Fear is our friend. Surely it is the reason we are here, right now. Evolutionarily speaking, it's the mother of survival. Unbridled fear, however, the fear that renders us immobile, is simply too much of a good thing. Our ability to harness the natural, raw energy that comes from a good dose of fear and propels us into action with intention is the impetus for change. This will be necessary to achieving your Fresh Start. Action with intention is the secret here because in the face of fear you get paralysis if you don't have good information on options. Imagine your primal ancestors, staring into a dark cave with nothing more than a big stick and a good-sized rock. Hungry, you know the cave could be home to the best meal you've eaten in weeks, and it might be just beyond the darkness. Then fear creeps in because it could also be home to a larger predator. The very real possibility that this could be the last cave you ever entered and the looming fact that your seed will never have the possibility to reproduce keeps you at a safe distance. What is missing? What is absent in this scenario that is producing this fear? <u>Reliable infor-mation from which intentional behavior would surely follow.</u>

While our ancestors fear was physical death, our fear is social and financial death (which you could argue is almost as concerning in our modern day). Financial death is just as likely to prohibit your ability to procreate and/or preserve the relationships you've already fostered.

You could argue that we are standing outside of a similar cave in the shadow of our ancestors. The decisions we make right now will affect our lives positively or negatively. How invaluable would the simple technology of blueprints for the cave, or, a census of what was in there, have been to our ancestors? Armed with appropriate knowledge, your "good fear" will give you the impetus to achieve your Fresh Start.

Realign Yourself with Your Fear

You may have heard it said, "Fear is simply False Evidence Appearing Real." While we can all think of situations where our fear was unwarranted, fears in the context of the distressed home owner are VERY true. It is our humble belief that, as a distressed home owner moving through this space to achieve a Fresh Start, we have to begin by realigning ourselves with our fear. Dismissing it as false evidence may work in many situations, but it might not serve us best here. Instead, let's identify with the fear and invite the 500-pound gorilla in the room with us to come forward. That's right; as uncomfortable and counterintuitive to our survival instincts as that may feel, by defining a worst-case scenario, we can begin to understand the resistance that could be holding our Fresh Start back. Jerry Ballanger says, "What's the best way to get rid of fear? Tear it apart."

At this point, some of you might know exactly what to do. You may have already done it and are using its value already. It may have been what put this book in your hand today. For the rest of us, follow this exercise to arrive at your FEAR.

Start with the simplest question possible and then get progressively harder. What you, like me, will find is that as each question is answered, the problem becomes more manageable. I don't need to tell you why managing your energy effectively from the start will help you in this journey to your Fresh Start because you already know that. I would like to suggest that you complete this exercise now and examine whether your perspective of your situation changes as a result.

Looking at the situation from multiple perspectives and allow yourself to arrive at what makes the most sense for your situation.

I've posed questions and offered suggestions to help you understand your thoughts and feelings. The main question is: What is important to you? You're welcome to use the other secondary questions as guides to dig deeper.

1. **What would happen if you did get this Fresh Start?**
   a. What's important about getting this Fresh Start, to you?
   b. What would the Fresh Start do for you that you don't already have?

2. **What would happen if you didn't get this Fresh Start?**
   a. Where would you go?
   b. What things would surely change for the worse as a result of not achieving a Fresh Start?
   c. Who else would be affected by these changes?
   d. What larger goals would also be affected?

3. **What wouldn't happen if I did get this Fresh Start?**
   a. Who/what am I saving?
   b. Is that what I really want? Or is that just what I think I really want?
   c. How would I know if that wasn't true?
   d. What evidence do I have to support these beliefs or the contrary?

4. **What wouldn't happen if I didn't get this Fresh Start?**

Summary: Reaction is based on instinct and intuition. Responding requires thoughtfulness. Initiating comes from imagination. An atmosphere where people can initiate can only come from a place where such a thing is encouraged.

Sara's Tip:

I did this exercise too late in my process. I was so motivated by my fear of the unknown that I just rushed into action as a remedy for my pain and fear. It wasn't until I had been told no twice by my lenders that I was introduced to this exercise. It's not what it did that affected my trajectory, as much as what it ended. After gaining some clarity around what my backup options were, my plans B, C, and even D, that I created some space around where I was and what my future held. This began the development of my inner game because without this clarity, I would never have been able to develop my vision. And it was the development of my vision, that included my worst-case scenario that channeled the focus of my power from an external means to an internal one. And, not surprisingly, that shift in my internal power also marked a shift in how my negotiations started going!

Key Mortgage Terms and Definitions

{20 Minutes}

. . .

In today's world just keeping up with the real estate terminology and jargon can be a full-time job! To help out, here are definitions of the most common real estate terms used today. If you haven't heard of some of them, don't worry because you probably will.

Please take a moment to review and understand the key terms you may hear when working with your mortgage lender or servicer. These can help you understand the process and make better decisions about your home loan and finances.

Mortgage: A legal document that pledges property to a lender as security for the repayment of the loan. The term also is used to refer to the loan itself.

Notice of Default (NOD): A notification given to a borrower stating that he or she has not made his or her payments by the predetermined deadline. It dictates that if the money owed (plus an additional legal fee) is not paid in a given time, the lender may choose to foreclose the borrower's property. Any other people who may be affected by the foreclosure may also receive a copy of the notification.

Mortgage Insurance: Insurance that protects lenders against losses caused by a borrower's default on a mortgage loan. Mortgage insurance (or MI) typically is required if the borrower's down payment is less than 20 percent of the purchase price.

Delinquency: Failure to make a payment when it is due. The condition of a loan when a scheduled payment has not been received by the due date but generally used to refer to a loan for which payment is thirty or more days past due.

Forbearance: The lender's postponement of legal action when a borrower is delinquent. It is usually granted when a borrower makes satisfactory arrangements to bring the overdue mortgage payments up to date.

Foreclosure Prevention: Steps by which the servicer works with the borrower to find a permanent solution to resolve an existing or impending loan delinquency.

Foreclosure: The legal process by which a property that is mortgaged as security for a loan may be sold and the proceeds of the sale applied to the mortgage debt. A foreclosure occurs when the loan becomes delinquent because payments have not been made or when the borrower is in default for a reason other than the failure to make timely mortgage payments.

Investor; The owner of the loan. These guys are behind the scenes, which means you will never speak with them.

Servicer: A firm that performs servicing functions, including collecting mortgage payments, paying the borrower's taxes and insurance, and generally managing borrower escrow accounts. This is who you send your payment to and communicate with.

Alternatives to Foreclosure

Repayment Plan: An arrangement by which a borrower agrees to make additional payments to pay down past due amounts while still making regularly scheduled payments.

Modification: Any change to the terms of a mortgage loan, including changes to the interest rate, loan balance, or loan term to help keep the home owner in the home.

Short Refinance: A short refinance, also known as a short payoff, is a transaction in which the current lender agrees to accept less than the full amount owed on your property. This process is similar to a short sale, but instead of the property being sold, it is refinanced with a new lender. The short refinance allows the home owner to retain ownership of the property, while avoiding a foreclosure or possible bankruptcy. Best of all it wipes out negative equity!

Short Sale: The process in which a servicer works with a delinquent borrower to sell the house by a realtor before the foreclosure sale.

Deed-in-Lieu: The transfer of title from a borrower to the lender to satisfy the mortgage debt and avoid foreclosure. Also called a voluntary conveyance. Basically you sign the title back over to the bank; these are rare.

www.ingramcontent.com/pod-product-compliance
Lightning Source LLC
Chambersburg PA
CBHW051540170526
45165CB00002B/812